DREAMS ARE ONLY
THE BEGINNING:

Becoming who you were meant to be

WORKBOOK

Original Text – 2002
Revised – 2011

By Dorothy A. Martin-Neville, PhD

Dedication

This book is dedicated to all those who have never had the chance to dream, to those who have been too afraid to dream, and to those whose dreams have been lost by the wayside.

May this workbook help you come to dream beyond your wildest expectations and may you come to see that there are no limits in this life other the ones you choose to create or accept.

You are the maker of your own dreams and the founder of your own journey. This book is provided to help you learn to live your life with the realization, and without a doubt, that this is an ever-unfolding, self-created experience that only you can direct.

There is nothing in this journey that can work against you. There are only challenges that cause you to become more than you have ever been.

Dreams are only the beginning of the process. So let's start from that awareness and see what great transformations take place within you as each dream you allow yourself to have comes alive continuously calling you to become even more than you were before. Create, enjoy, and grow!

With love and blessings,

Dorothy

Contents

CHAPTER ONE

CHILDHOOD

Dreams are the gifts we give ourselves. They are a necessity not a luxury because they are the gifts that make everything possible. Without dreams there is nothing to take us any further than the place where we are right now, physically, emotionally, and spiritually. That would be an impossibility since like a rose we are not meant to be stagnant, to stand still, but to continue to blossom throughout the journey.

Without acknowledging our own dreams and acting upon them we subtly, or not-so-subtly, become someone else's creation. We end up living someone else's dreams with no room in our lives for us. It is as if no one has ever given us the right to exist, including us. That is such an unhealthy and yet, sadly, common occurrence.

Many young children begin their dream history in wishing for a brother or sister. Some begin with a wish for a special present whether for a holiday or a birthday. They go to sleep dreaming about the gift, to the point where it almost seems real – until it is. Their faith in dreaming begins with that experience.

Unfortunately some children are told not to dream. They are told that their dreams will only get them into trouble or that they will never come true so why bother? Others have been told that their dreams are selfish; their parents are doing the best they can and they should learn to be satisfied with what they have and where they are. Some are told to never wish for or expect more.

For all those children, and so many more this workbook provides a way for you to reclaim your life, reclaim your dreams, and most definitely, reclaim all that you are meant to be. If no one has ever given you permission to exist you now have it with all my blessings – permission to exist AND permission to dream and dream BIG.

I believe our dreams are truly our soul's way of guiding us to the next step. They are our soul's way of showing us where we need to go next, what we need to do, and what we need to learn. As a surprise to many, our soul speaks so much louder than our head or our mouth; it is simply that we have learned not to listen and as a result we may not even remember that it is talking to us.

Relearn how to hear what your soul has to say through answering the questions in each section of this book. Each question is meant to help you reclaim what you may have forgotten, what you may have put aside, and what you need to bring into the light. Take the time you need for reflection, if it is required, to answer each question in whatever order works for you and in whatever sections work for you. This is a gift, not a test.

This book is about you. It is about you coming home again to enjoy your truth, your vision and your life. Life is meant to be filled with passion, vitality, and joy, as well as with an unlimited number of dreams. I have discovered that dreams can transform your life instantly even before they are actualized. Just by allowing yourself to dream you can transform your daily life. In an instant! Just the creativity and the adventure of the dream can bring you alive.

The excitement, freedom, joy and self-discovery that come with having dreams give you back your love of life and your love of you. You begin to live a life of gratitude, hope and motivation. It may not always be easy but it is always simple. Let's help you get there. To begin, answer these questions:

- As a young child were you allowed to dream?
- Was it encouraged?
- Were you able to share those dreams with those you lived with?
- What was said about them? About you?

Take a few moments to reflect even further on your childhood. Write down:

- What you remember about your dreams.
- What they were.
- What became of them.

This will allow you to understand where your present day beliefs come from. It will also allow you to see how much respect and creativity you once gave to those dreams and to yourself.

_____

_____

_____

_____

_____

_____

_____

When you were little, did you have dreams about being someone else?

- Did you wish you lived somewhere else?
- What part of your life did you wish was different?

_____

_____

_____

_____

_____

_____

_____

_____

_____

_____

_____

_____

_____

_____

_____

_____

_____

_____

_____

_____

_____

_____

_____

_____

_____

_____

_____

- What did you want to be when you grew up?
- Did it happen? If not, why?

_____

_____

_____

_____

_____

_____

_____

_____

_____

_____

_____

_____

_____

_____

_____

_____

_____

_____

_____

_____

_____

_____

_____

_____

_____

_____

_____

_____

- Once you started school, did you feel that you belonged to the "right" crowd?
- If not, what did you do to change that?
- Or did you just give up and accept that you would never belong any where? That you would never fit in?
- Or, finally, did you create your own crowd, believing that if you couldn't get what you wanted in one place you could simply create it in another?

_____

_____

_____

_____

_____

_____

_____

_____

_____

_____

_____

_____

_____

_____

_____

_____

_____

_____

_____

_____

_____

_____

Look at your dreams and wants as a child:

- Did you believe that you needed to accept things as they were, or did you believe that if you can dream it, if you can taste it, you can make it real?
- Did you ever reach the point of making what you wanted happen? If so, how?

_____
_____
_____
_____
_____
_____
_____
_____
_____
_____
_____
_____
_____
_____
_____
_____
_____
_____
_____
_____
_____
_____
_____
_____
_____
_____

_____

_____

_____

_____

_____

_____

_____

_____

_____

_____

_____

_____

_____

_____

_____

_____

_____

_____

_____

_____

_____

_____

_____

_____

_____

_____

_____

_____

_____

- As a young child, did you have dreams about your adolescence?
- What were they? Did they come true?

_____
_____
_____
_____
_____
_____
_____
_____
_____
_____
_____
_____
_____
_____
_____
_____
_____
_____
_____
_____
_____
_____
_____
_____
_____
_____
_____
_____

Chapter Two

Adolescence

One of the most difficult aspects of adolescence is that you usually have no idea who you are, where you belong or even where you are going. All of life seems to be an uncertain mystery and yet you are expected to be focused enough to do good, get good grades and be pleasant to all those around you. It is quite a dilemma. You probably got so many messages even mixed messages at that point in your life that you may have forgotten where the messages came from or what the purpose of them actually was.

It may be important for you to question where you learned the most impactful messages or beliefs you hold. Was it from a parent? Teacher? Friend? Stranger? Media? Your own deductive reasoning? Knowing this can allow you to put the beliefs in perspective.

As an example, have you decided, or been taught, that if someone doesn't return a call within a few hours, that they don't really like you? If that is the case, and it happens to you, then logically you should immediately drop them from your friendship circle. However, as an adult you may know that they really do like you – and also know that they can be so busy some days that they don't have a chance to return your call and/or they have so many folks needing something from them that they can't take the time to just sit, talk, and relax with you which is their real desire.

You are now forced to choose to either let go of the old belief which doesn't fit what you know to be factual at this point in your life and embrace a new understanding of friendship or you must release this person from your life, forever. It is important to recognize that when you find yourself caught with two or more perspectives on the same subject such as in this case that you can easily become stuck in a world of confusion, pain, and mixed messages, oblivious as to why you have such powerful yet contradictory messages running in your mind.

The truth is that this is often a consequence of your adolescent years when you were taught social values as if there was one universal set of "right" values for everyone. You internalized them fully, often without realizing it. In addition, as I show below, you also internalized beliefs and messages concerning who you were and qualities you possessed or did not possess. As an adult, your experience may tell you that those old values and or beliefs were not actually correct either.

It is now time to let go of the confusion and uncertainly of adolescence and become a self-defined adult who has permission to dream, to see the world, and yourself, through your own eyes, your own experiences, and your own truths. It's time to be you. Sometimes that simply happens by facing one contradictory set of beliefs at a time.

When I was in elementary school, my "future" dream was to be a Rockette. I loved to dance and wanted to do it professionally. I had taken tap, ballet, and jazz and it was the wild, fun, alive and yet choreographed dancing that touched my soul. The Rockettes seemed to me to be the perfect answer. I found a dream that would carry me through many difficult times. In my mind's eye, they danced with all their passion and with their souls while also being synchronized with the world around them. There were times when that dream was all I had to hold onto. It was the dream that would get me out of that town and give me the life I wanted more than anything in the world. It was going to be glamorous, fun, and a life of independence yet in a tight knit community.

On the other side of my brain was my mother's message that I was too lazy to be Rockette since they needed to work hard and practice for long hours. Although, as the oldest girl I had a large degree of responsibility very early, I also had a message that said I was not capable of hard work. Which was the truth? What was I honestly capable of? At times I did feel lazy, I didn't want to move, so perhaps my mother was right. At other times I was full of dreams, ambitions, energy, and vibrancy so perhaps she was wrong.

Regardless of whether she was right or wrong, without that dream my life would have been far more difficult that it was. I held onto the dream but came to lose faith that I would ever be able to achieve it because of the message about who I was. That was a message that stayed with me for years, about many things, despite what I accomplished. When fact contradicted the belief – the belief won. This really was contradiction at its most powerful and most destructive...

I didn't have dreams about school during adolescence. School was simply what you had to do so I did it. I was good at it. Good grades came easily so I never gave them much thought. School was what I tolerated on the way to really living life which would come later, hopefully as a Rockette.

The truth of what actually happened was that I did not become a Rockette and academic studies became immensely enriching and important to me. School became so much more than just getting good grades. I became involved in civil rights and I have never been the same since. I was asked to debate, speaking in front of the whole class, about Martin Luther King's position. My teachers were life-giving and life-saving. They were gifts beyond words. They created other messages and gave me hope that as hard working as I was, and they accepted me as being, I could qualify for college and change my life. Who was I to believe? Would I be betraying either side if I chose to accept the other perspective? Who was I willing to betray?

Some of my friends needed to try some dreams on for size and they needed to, or chose to, explore a variety of dreams. It was like taking on different identities. I admired their ability and willingness to do so. That was the only way for them to discover what fit and so they did it. Some dreams they could try on for a few days and know that they didn't work at all. Some they tried on for a year or so.

For myself, I remember my Dad insisting often during the high school years that I not get too big for my britches. I was supposed to follow the game plan of all those who had walked before me. For me that meant I was suppose to get good grades in high school and immediately afterwards marry a man with a good, solid job that would always be needed, such as an electrician, a plumber or a policeman.

My father wanted me to give him 20 grandchildren. He wanted a larger family and it was my job to get married and provide it for him. To prove I hadn't gotten too big for my britches and to fulfill his dream I would have to stay in the projects where I "belonged". If I did that, however, and a part of me liked the idea of marrying immediately, there would probably be no room for any other dreams I may have had. If my next dream proved to be different from his, I would have to make a choice as to whose dreams I would follow- his or mine.

At that point it was imperative to know what my dreams and thoughts were and what my expectations and hopes for the future were as well. It wasn't until my senior year however that I was ready to really look at what the cost would be for me to be that defined, to have a dream that was solely mine, and to believe I could achieve it.

In a very different format, during my daughter's adolescence she decided she was going to be a doctor. However, after seeing so many female doctors leaving their children with a series of nannies she dropped the idea. Then for about a year she was going to be a lawyer. She loved the power of persuading someone to see things her way or of convincing someone to behave differently. Her ability to present an argument was well developed from years of experience at home and she felt that arena would allow her to do it on a regular and paid basis.

Finally, she recognized the strength of her need to heal others. She needed to help the people most in need while having the time to raise her own children herself. She wanted to be home each evening, to eat with them, to love them, and to help them when needed. After trying on all the varied hats, she decided to become a pediatric nurse practitioner. It gave her the best of all her dreams, while allowing her the lifestyle she wanted.

How many of you had the luxury of exploring various dreams? Look at your pattern in dreaming; there always is one. Discover yours in order to determine its strengths and limitations. Learn about you from it. That way you can change your patterns if warranted and you will be able to see how and why you have succeeded or failed at creating the life you want.

- Did you know to look at the best of all your dreams and come up with a compilation of the best of each?
- In dreaming about your life, did you have a choice?

_____

_____

_____

_____

_____

_____

_____

_____

_____

_____

_____

_____
_____
_____
_____
_____
_____
_____
_____
_____
_____
_____
_____
_____
_____
_____
_____
_____
_____
_____
_____
_____
_____
_____
_____
_____
_____
_____
_____

- Did you ever really look at what you wanted to do with your life?
- How well thought-out were your dreams?
- What did you do to make them happen?
- Did you keep your dreams "realistic"?
- Did you stop yourself from dreaming "too big" because you might never reach your goals?
- Did you limit your dreams so that they wouldn't make another feel inadequate?
- Did you settle for less? If so, why?

_____

_____

_____

_____

_____

_____

_____

_____

_____

_____

_____

_____

_____

_____

_____

_____

_____

_____

_____

Dorothy A. Martin-Neville, PhD

_____

_____

_____

_____

_____

_____

_____

_____

_____

_____

_____

_____

_____

_____

_____

_____

_____

_____

_____

_____

_____

_____

_____

_____

_____

_____

_____

_____

_____

_____

Finally, without any self-judgment at all:

- Did you find a way to sabotage yourself or your dreams out of fear?
- How did you do that?
- What was your fear?
- What did you think would have happened if you didn't?

It is important to understand because these beliefs could be affecting you now.

_____

_____

_____

_____

_____

_____

_____

_____

_____

_____

_____

_____

_____

_____

_____

_____

_____

_____

_____

_____

_____

_____

Chapter Three

Our Early Steps into Adulthood

Immediately after high school, many of us thought of ourselves as being grown-up, at least we tried to.

We were still young and unprepared for what was to follow. Nonetheless, many of us began pretending that we understood the world and that we were OK. It was a period of getting our feet on the ground. We had waited for that special day for what felt like forever.

Some went to college. In that scenario there was more freedom and more independence yet there was still the environment of school that kept us safe in some ways. It allowed us to play grown up while still being led by others. We still had teachers telling us what to study, although we chose when we would do that. We still had school vacations although, many of us worked at that time. Some of us had majors picked by our parents, even schools picked by our parents. We were independent, yet not.

Others went to work right out of high school. Some had always known what they wanted to do and did it. Some were told by their parents what they would do. It may have been to work in the family business or whatever else the family needed.

Some got married right after high school, if they even finished. Immediately they were expected to know how to create a good family life, how to run a household, and/or how to support a family.

Whatever the situation, it was new. The circumstances were new as well. We were not just beginning the next phase of our lives; we were beginning the first steps in following our dreams or, of avoiding them, as well.

Depending upon your age at this very moment, those years may seem like a lifetime ago or perhaps just a very long time ago. Regardless, that was a very crucial time for those of us who had dreams and who wanted to know how they would fit into our lives. We needed to learn how to make them come true. We needed to begin taking risks and paying the price. Rarely is the largest cost of a dream about money as we would discover.

Dreams require us to give up outdated self-images. They require us to give up old beliefs that may have held us back. Above all, they require us to take risks. The require us to become clear, focused and specific about what is needed to make our dreams come true. As adults, we cannot simply sit there and talk about our dreams, waiting for someone else to tell us what to do or how to make them happen. Our dreams are OUR responsibility. Our dreams are OUR vision. We are the only one who can see them clearly. As a result, we are the only one who can make them come true.

That takes an investment in time and energy, and a willingness to do both the outer work, as well as to make the inner changes needed to make our dreams come true. It means looking at those parts of ourselves that want someone else to rescue us, or to do the hard parts. It means looking at those parts of ourselves that want to whine and blame someone else for it being so hard. It also means looking at those parts of ourselves that want to believe everyone else has it easy; everyone else gets what they want without effort.

In addition, it means looking at those parts of our personality that want to tell others how to do all the work while we just sit back waiting to feel proud of "our" accomplishments. Having a dream and making it come true requires us to own it as ours. It requires us to be so committed that nothing gets in our way. Some things may slow us down. Some things may distract us for a bit but nothing can cause us to lose sight of that dream, that vision which comes from our soul. That would require personal choice since losing sight of the dream would mean losing sight of who we are. As a result, there would be a part of us that would never be actualized that would always remain unfulfilled. Know the difference: replacing a dream can be a result of growth; losing a dream is a result of fear.

- What dreams did you have when you left high school?
- What did you do with them?
- Did you replace them, lose them, or create them?
- If you didn't create a dream, did another dream take its place or did you give up?
- Did you lose you?

_____
_____
_____
_____
_____

- What have you learned about your dreams so far?
- How do you see your dreams?
- Do you allow yourself to have any?

_____

_____

_____

_____

_____

_____

_____

_____

_____

_____

_____

_____

_____

_____

_____

_____

_____

_____

_____

_____

_____

_____

_____

_____

_____

_____

_____

_____

It is easy to forget that regardless of what dream you have, it means NOT having the opposite. Have you thought about that? If your dream is to be married, it means you will not be single. If it is to have children, it means that you will no longer be without the responsibility for others. If you like your independence, it means you are no longer solely in charge of your time. Having ANYTHING requires giving something else up. Going back to college means giving up free time. It may mean giving up the chance to make an immediate paycheck. It may mean giving up some other interests.

Before you make a choice, before you create a dream make sure you look at it closely. Look at what it requires. Look at what it asks of you, to the best of your ability. Dreams deserved to be looked at from all angles possible. They deserve to have your full commitment.

- Are you willing to pay the price for your dream?
- Is it worth it to you?

_____
_____
_____
_____
_____
_____
_____
_____
_____
_____
_____
_____
_____

_____

_____

_____

_____

_____

_____

_____

_____

_____

_____

_____

_____

_____

_____

_____

_____

_____

_____

_____

_____

_____

_____

_____

_____

_____

_____

_____

- Before you commit - are you ready?
- Can you follow it without resentment, without blame towards another, regardless of outcome?
- What are your priorities?
- Is the dream worth the cost?
- Is it worth what you are giving up?
- What is your dream at this moment?
- What does it require of you?

_____

_____

_____

_____

_____

_____

_____

_____

_____

_____

_____

_____

_____

_____

_____

_____

_____

_____

_____

_____

_____

_____

A Linda Ronstadt song says that THE IMPOSSIBLE JUST TAKES A LITTLE TIME. Sometimes our dreams feel impossible. Is that an excuse you have used to justify giving your dreams up? Feeling like a victim, feeling powerless is an excuse many folks use to avoid following their dreams. It is their way of justifying their lack of willingness to invest in their lives. It's their way of explaining away their own self-hatred and their lack of faith in themselves. When you feel stuck look at why.

What freedoms are you too frightened to consider? A move because you will not know anyone? A breakup because you are too frightened of being alone? A relationship because you are too frightened of being hurt? A commitment because it may not be the "right" choice? An ultimatum because you may not like the answer? If so, your fears are preventing you from claiming all that you can be. They are preventing you from moving ahead on your journey.

You will ALWAYS land on your feet if you jump with integrity. If the dream doesn't turn out the way you wanted it to, if it doesn't feel or look the way you thought it would, what did you learn from it? Life is a process. That dream was only a step along the way. It was a life lesson, a preparation, a gift of learning you brought in to teach yourself things you never would have learned otherwise. Whether it was everything you wanted or not, you now need to ask yourself "How have I grown?" "What have I learned?"

When you create a dream, while it is still a dream, you are nonetheless still called to grow in so many ways. By the time the dream is actualized, you have grown and changed in so many ways that you are not the person who created the dream. You are so much more. That could actually be one of the reasons a dream didn't work, if that is the case. You may have outgrown it before it was even fully completed.

The dream was a gift yet it was only the beginning of discovering you. You have such great potential that it requires more than just one dream and more than just one vision to be actualized. That is why after a period of time even when we achieve a dream we may want to expand it, to change it or to move on from it. We are no longer at the same level as when the dream first began. Amazingly, we always know when it is time to move.

When we know in our hearts and in our souls when something is no longer right for us, we need to listen to that knowing. When we don't, we are choosing to live in self-betrayal. We thus loose our experience of inner peace; we lose our sense of being right where we belong, because we no longer are. If we live in our truth, we know when it is time for another dream or time to expand the one we have achieved, developing it even further, taking it to another level. I firmly believe that when we choose not to listen to what is right for us we are choosing self-hatred and self-denial.

We are embodied souls. Our souls live inside of these physical forms we carry around with us. Our souls are filled with wisdom and self-understanding. They speak to us through those feelings, those body senses that tell us what to do and what not to do. We know when it is time to move on and we also know if moving on is a way of running away, from ourselves and our growth.

We know the difference. We just don't always want to listen to what we know.

- In what way are you currently not listening to what you know is your truth?
- What area of you life is requiring change that you are avoiding?
- Why are you?

_____
_____
_____
_____
_____
_____
_____
_____
_____
_____
_____
_____
_____
_____
_____
_____
_____
_____
_____
_____
_____
_____
_____
_____
_____

Chapter Four

The Spirituality of Our Dreams

As embodied souls, we are intrinsically spiritual beings. I believe we have come into this world with very specific areas of growth to achieve. I believe as well that in those areas in which we are meant to grow the most we produce the gifts that we have chosen to bring to the world, to our world task. We did not come here just to take; we came here to give back as well. That is the only way this world will be transformed. That responsibility of transformation belongs to each of us.

As we grow, we have more wisdom to share with others and many more skills. I believe that because we are spiritual beings we are meant to live a contemplative life style. Because we are physical beings, we are meant to live in community. Combining these two objectives requires the constant search for balance that we all need. Sometimes 80% community involvement and 20% contemplation works for us. At another point in our life, 80% contemplation and 20% community action is what is needed. We need to know which is which. We can only learn that in prayer, a much forgotten commodity.

We come in with a personal need to grow, to come into self-awareness and self-love. We do that by learning to listen to the inner life. It amazes me how much we can get caught up in the fast pace, in the tools of avoidance such as busyness, workaholic tendencies, substance abuse, over involvement in too many activities, even in good deeds. We can all find ways to avoid alone times; to avoid the quiet that allows us to reconnect with ourselves. I believe we came in with a natural skill of talking to our own souls and of being spoken to in return. Somehow, in the rush to be important or in the need to belong we can easily lose that connection to ourselves.

The quiet times, the meditation times, the reflection times, all allow us to come home, to come back to ourselves. I know many who are afraid of those times. They avoid them as if they are dangerous. It is in those times however that we most clearly hear what we need to hear and that we then discover our innermost dreams.

The dreams we have, the dreams that come from our soul, are the soul's way of showing us what we need to do next to take us to the next step in our journey. The dreams that connect us to our passion, to our life force, to our profound inner joy, are the dreams we have come here to accomplish. They are the dreams that take us where we need to go in order to be the most of who we are meant to be.

Sometimes they seen too impossible, too difficult, or we feel too alone to accomplish anything. It is at those times when we most need to remember, as Nelson Mandela so clearly points out, that we are children of God. We are the precious children of an all-loving God. It is a God who has walked every step of the way with us.

In my experience, one of the things that can make change and decision-making so difficult is the belief that we are in this all alone. When we lose sight of our truth, of our spiritual lives, we can easily come to think that we are walking alone on this planet, unnoticed, unimportant, and unnecessary since we don't even have us.

For decades, literally, I have kept the prayer FOOTPRINTS in my wallet. Although I know it by heart, I cherish the opportunity to take it out on occasion to read it and remind myself of my dearest friend along the journey, my "proof" that I am not alone. It goes like this:

FOOTPRINTS

One night a man had a dream. He dreamed he was walking along the beach with the LORD. Across the sky flashed scenes from his life. For each scene, he noticed two sets of footprints in the sand, one belonging to him, and the other to the LORD.

When the last scene of his life flashed before him, he looked back at the footprints in the sand. He noticed many times along the path of life there was only one set of footprints. He also noticed that it happened at the very lowest and saddest times of his life.

This really bothered him and he questioned the LORD about it. "LORD, you said that once I decided to follow you, you'd walk with me all the way. But I noticed that during the most troublesome times in my life there is only one set of footprints. I don't understand why, when I needed you most, you would leave me."

The LORD replied, "My precious, precious child. I love you and I would never leave you. During those times of trial and suffering, when you see only one set of footprints, it was then that I was carrying you."

Author Unknown

We always walk with God and that is shown to us often if we allow ourselves to see. I do not believe in accidents or coincidences. "Coincidences" are God's way of showing us that we are not alone. They show us that we are always guided, always watched over, and always protected. It is like the story of Palm Sunday in the Scriptures. When we decide to get up, to get on the donkey (and doesn't it seem like most dreams take forever?) and to go into town, all the guides and angels clear the path for us to go forward. They get all the debris out of the way. We must first make the decision to follow the dream however. We alone must make that choice. We have total freewill to do so or not. Once we believe however and jump in, faith can move mountains and you will find that yet again the impossible has occurred, another everyday miracle.

Notice that the person we could never meet happens to walk across our path. The money we could never get comes in a loan or a grant we never knew about, and so on and so on and so on. If you are willing to see how watched over you have been, how protected and guided you always are, simply look at your history.

- What "miracles' took place in your life?
- What "impossibilities" became possible?

Be open and write about them:

_____

_____

_____

_____

_____

_____

_____

_____

_____

_____

_____

_____

_____

_____

_____

_____

_____

_____

_____

_____

_____

_____

_____

_____

_____

_____

_____

_____

_____

- How many times have you "known": something wouldn't work and yet it did?

_____

_____

_____

_____

_____

_____

_____

_____

_____

_____

_____

_____

_____

_____

_____

_____

_____

_____

_____

_____

_____

_____

_____

_____

_____

_____

_____

- How many times has the outcome exceeded your expectations?
- In what way?
- What do you think caused that to happen?

_____

_____

_____

_____

_____

_____

_____

_____

_____

_____

_____

_____

_____

_____

_____

_____

_____

_____

_____

_____

_____

_____

_____

_____

Never have you had to undergo anything alone. If you didn't feel the presence of God it is because you didn't choose to. It is because you have learned to ignore what you know on a soul level. You may have been too caught up in a victim mentality or in anger or defiance to listen. When you get caught up in mind games with yourself, or in blaming others, you lose your ability to feel the Presence. You can get so busy thinking about your problems, or how hard life is, or how no one is there for you, that you cannot see what is right in front of you. What a loss.

Remember, we already know the answers, we already know what we need and we already know what is right or wrong for us. We just need to learn to listen. Equally important is the need to see the work of God in our lives every single day. That doesn't mean we always get what we want. It does mean, however, that we always get what is best for us. We have the freedom to refuse it whenever we want. Because we are never left alone, we will get another chance, later, when we are ready. If it is something we have come here to do, we will be given everything we need to make it happen, more than once if necessary.

We can make it difficult or not. We have the power to do that to ourselves. But do we always need to use it??? Be nice to yourself, enjoy the trip. We are meant to live life, not survive it. Dreams are what take us from surviving to living because our dreams are what lead us to what we came here to achieve.

Many of us intentionally give up our dreams in the illusion that if we love another we must give up our dreams and support them in following theirs. That is not love; it is dependency and enmeshment. We did not come here to survive while we help another thrive. We did not come here to solely be a support system to others. We came here because we had personal work to do for ourselves. We have dreams to live that belong only to us. In living our dreams, we give others the example that it is good for them to follow their dreams as well. We teach best by modeling healthy behavior. It isn't an "either-or". In relationship it is "both." Each one in a relationship needs to know and honor their dreams while supporting the other in living theirs.

Sometimes our dreams may be similar to another's. If that is the case, then we can work together to create the united dream. It is so very important to remember, however, that you are two very different people. There will be aspects of that dream that are all yours. There will be qualities in that dream that are only yours. Do not lose sight of them. By trying too hard to have identical dreams with another, you may both lose your dream and each other as well. The dream may be similar but you two are not. Do not lose yourself. Keep your unique approach, your unique perspective to this dream, this vision, simply share it with the other – but do not surrender it. When you do, everyone loses.

I have seen so many people come to me in my office, male and female who got lost in the actualizing of their dream. They gave so much of themselves away in order to appear easy going or loving that the dream ceased to be a reflection of them. We owe it to ourselves, to our loved ones and to the world to save room for us in our lives and in our dreams. Giving all that up isn't love. It is at best a lack of self-worth and at worst a form of self-hatred.

Know your dream. In the quiet of each evening go within in silence to find out if you made room for you today. Discover if you gave away a part of you today. Did you give it to your children? Your employer? Your employees? Your friends? Your business partner? Your schedule?

Being pliable is not the same as ceasing to exist. YOU are the gift you bring to others. Your work is a reflection of you if you let it be. YOU must exist before your dream can. You are the reason you came here; let you shine. Following your dreams is what makes it all possible. They are the vehicle through which the world gets to see the best of who you are. Let your soul out, the world needs it.

So many come to believe they are selfish, even narcissistic, if they have a dream that is solely theirs. That is not true. If you believe your dream is the **only** dream of value, yes narcissism has crept in. However, if you are in relationship and you take turns actualizing your dreams because of time or financial reasons, then that is love, compassion and teamwork.

If you give yours up totally however so another can have theirs then the relationship will eventually pay the price because there is no longer space for what makes you who you are and calls you to become even more. In that instance there is only room for one person in the relationship and you aren't the one. Knowing the difference between compromise and surrender is so important to be in a healthy relationship, with yourself and another.

Chapter Five

Dreams are Sequential:
One Follows the Other

Many of us grew up thinking that once we had one dream, once we achieved it, we lived only that one dream throughout our lives. We were taught to believe that you got one job and stayed with it forever. You worked for one company and stayed there until you retired. You had one relationship and it lasted for life. Fortunately, or unfortunately, for many of us, none of those things have been true.

At the beginning of high school, I wanted to be "rich" and live in a tenement. After living in the projects for most of my life, I thought that one family having a whole floor of a house to itself was the epitome of wealth. Knowing that I could achieve that gave me hope. By the time I was old enough to live that dream however it had changed. It had served a purpose though; it gave me hope when I needed it.

As a senior, I wanted to be of service to others. My parents would not send girls to college so being a social worker was not an option. Since our high was in the inner city and unaccredited, my second choice of nursing school was not an option either since they could not take me. The only way I knew to live my dream of service at a higher level was to enter the convent and become a Catholic nun. So I did just that. It was my dream and I wanted to live it.

What that showed me is that dreams are a reflection of where we are in our lives. Dreams come as we are ready for them. As we grow, so do they. We never have only one dream in a lifetime. Life is too full and we are too multi-dimensional to be that limited. We need to be open to listening and following our dreams as they come to us. They call us to grow to each new step. They tell us it is time to become more of who we are meant to be and to reflect that for the world to see.

Religious life, an uncharacteristic choice, proved to be a gift beyond words. Nonetheless, many told me not to do it, not to go there. They said I wouldn't stay. They said I didn't belong there. They said I was too alive, that I would die in that place. If I had listened to them I would have missed out on the most nurturing, the most grounding and the most self-defining period of my life. I knew I needed to go there. I knew in my heart and soul that there was something there for me. Something I needed that could only be found there and I needed it badly. I didn't know what that was; I just knew I needed to go there to get it. What a gift beyond words those years were for me. As I look back now, I can see that those years transformed me. They gave me back to me. Dreams that we know we need to follow are like that. They give us our truth. They form us, regardless of how others feel about them.

- How many times have you not followed a dream because others doubted its validity or its permanence?

_____

_____

_____

_____

_____

_____

_____

_____

_____

_____

_____

_____

_____

_____

_____

_____

_____

_____

_____

_____

_____

_____

_____

_____

_____

_____

_____

_____

_____

_____

_____

_____

I believe there are many times when turning to others for direction or guidance in the pragmatics of living your dreams is a great and necessary idea. I never believe, however, in asking others if you should follow your dreams. Have you noticed that it is those people who will not follow their own dreams who work so arduously to convince you not to follow yours? Do you see the connection?

Those people who are too frightened to follow their own dreams are not going to advise you to go forward. Why would they? Where would they get the faith in you or in your life to believe that all things are possible if they don't have it for themselves? If you want advice about following your dreams, turn to someone who has followed theirs. Doesn't that make sense?

Notice as well that each dream you get builds on the one before it. Have you noticed that each dream you follow teaches you something or develops something in you that is necessary for the next dream you have?

- In what way have your past dreams prepared you for the new dream?
- What qualities in you needed to be developed beforehand so that you could then be able to move forward?

_____
_____
_____
_____
_____
_____
_____

In seeing that they build on each other, we can give up the illusion that any dream we have had was a mistake, or a failure. Each was necessary for the next. An old Chinese proverb says that it is the great man who has failed many times, for it means he has tried many times. He has lived his life fully not simply put in his time. Each dream is a preparation for the next, so treat it accordingly. Treat each dream as a precious calling from within. It is your soul's way of saying ""OK, we are ready to move on. We are ready to continue becoming." What a gift!

Chapter Six

Relationships and Marriage

As a psychotherapist for over 25 year and as a woman who has lived a full life herself, I have seen many dreams about relationships and marriage that are based on illusion rather than reality. It happens because one or both parties had a dream, a vision, of who their perfect partner would be and they insisted on finding that dream-whether it was realistic or not- or ready or not.

When that is the case and we don't allow our dream to evolve naturally, we will always find that the dream collapses sooner or later. I believe that has a great deal to do with the extraordinarily high divorce rate we now have. In a changing world where we are told we can have it all, we can easily come to expect that we and our partners be it all. Our humanity, the reality that we are beings in process, continuously growing but never fully completed, is disregarded and replaced with the expectations of a completed package, as if we were buying a car not joining with another embodied soul on a journey we are going to walk together. It sets us up with unfair expectations for ourselves and others.

Most of us enter relationships with the hope that they will last forever. Once we take the risk of loving someone completely, and are told that we are loved in return, we become filled with great hope and expectation for what this relationship can become.

If it is to work, however, we need to be honest with ourselves and with our partner about what our expectations for this relationship are, as well as what our individual needs and wants are. Once talked about we need to discuss whether or not they are being met.

If we acknowledge what is happening –being open to seeing things as they are- we will come to see whether or not our needs and expectations are realistic and whether or not our partner is even interested in meeting them.

We also get to see how realistic our partner's needs and expectations are for us, as well as the relationship. Only once these elements are looked at are we totally capable of assessing if this relationship can go forward either into marriage or a long term committed connection.

I am a romantic and an optimist. I have seen marriages that have worked. I have seen partners who were still in love many years later – still laughing, enjoying and flirting with their partners.

For those who have made it, it required that they be honest with each other and that they see their partner for who they were and who they weren't. They were able to adjust their expectations accordingly, giving each other room to grow as they changed and evolved over time. They had mutual respect and permission for the other to become who they were called to be, keeping some mystery and excitement in the relationship. There was little to no sense of ownership or control. That environment allowed the relationship to stay fresh.

When you accept that relationships cause you to grow in ways being alone never could, you recognize that in a relationship all of your strengths and limitations will be mirrored back at you. You can blame your partner for that or simply accept that you aren't done growing yet and that no matter who you were in relationship with your limitations would be there with you.

It is in relationship that you truly learn to love in a real embodied way. You learn to love yourself and accept your own craziness and you learn as well to take your partners craziness as just a part of who they are, without blame or resentment. You may even find yourselves laughing at times at how you have managed to survive as crazy as we all are. Nonetheless, having taken the risk of loving and growing in the process, you see what an amazing, even if imperfect, experience the gift of loving and being loved is, regardless of the outcome.

The dream, the hope, to have a partner is a natural part of us, and an important part of our growth. When we find someone who can call us forward and who can teach us about loving and being in love, which has the power to convince us to take that risk, actually allowing that love to unfold provides us with an experience that is rich beyond measure.

To work, however, our relationships have to be based on reality. No relationship comes with a guarantee but the best chance for one surviving comes when it is solid and grounded. One example of an ungrounded relationship which is set up to fail that I share often in class and at seminars is when someone, as I said above, forms an image of the perfect person, the perfect lover, and the perfect partner and that image is exactly what s/he expects to marry-with no variations. When they start dating someone and they decide this is the one, they only allow themselves to see the expected perfection. When that "perfect person" is late for a date the dreamer will say "He (or she) is so important and has so many demands on him, he couldn't help it."

When this person stands them up again and again they will say "It must have been important or a crisis since I know that more than anything in the world s/he wanted to be here." And so it goes... Friends may have a very different picture but they are told that they don't understand or that they don't see what the dreamer sees.

For the individual involved to see it any other way would mean that perhaps this "perfect partner" isn't perfect. Consequently, they would have to start all over again looking for that perfect being but their need to be in a relationship is too great to allow that. As a result, excuses, justifications, and rationalizations become a way of life. These justifications are easier to accept than the humanity or limitations of their partner, or of their vision.

After years of marriage, or of living together, almost inevitably one person starts to grow. The lateness, the no-shows, and all the other disrespectful or abusive behavior patterns come to be seen differently. The excuses, justifications and rationalizations stop. Somehow the perfect partner is seen as no long being the person he or she married. It is said that he or she has changed. In fact, he or she hasn't changed at all but has remained exactly the same because there was no reason to change. That is only part of the problem.

The growing partner has started to live in reality and to see the lifestyle that has been justified for years. The wants and needs that were not being met are finally acknowledged. For that to occur, the aware partner has actually had to begin to grow in self-love and can now recognize the right to have their needs and wants met. S/he is now ready to live in reality and be honest with herself and him.

Only at this point, finally, is there even the remotest chance of this relationship working. Only at this point is there a chance that they could develop something between them. This entire time at least one partner has been in love with an illusion. He or she never married their partner; they married an illusion of who they wanted their partner to be. The dreamer hasn't been betrayed; their partner has. They presented who they were and yet their partner never saw them. They have been invisible to their partner this whole time believing they were loved when in fact they were never even seen.

For the first time, they now have a chance at a relationship that is real not an illusion. NOW there is the chance to look at who each has married, to see the great qualities that actually exist as well as the limitations. They now have a history, and a chance to see what needs to change to support going forward and to see if they truly want to be married to their partner as well as seeing if they are both willing to make this work but this time falling in love with who their partner really is.

For some, with great effort, it finally comes to work and in ways that are far beyond their wildest dreams. It becomes in reality their dream relationship, far better and more fulfilling than the illusion s/he was trying to live.

For some others, it becomes clear they are not matched well at all and they need to move on. This was a life lesson that allowed each of them to see what it is they needed to learn about themselves and about how they do relationship. It was an opportunity for tremendous growth if they are willing to grow from it. It provided far greater awareness of who they are as well as of how they do relationship with everyone.

If they move on consciously, and in awareness of themselves, they are taking into their next relationship far more skills than they brought into this previous one. Because of this, it wasn't a failing or a mistake but another gift, as painful as it was.

It is when you believe that you are not lovable or that you will never find a partner that you tend to create illusions. You want that perfect love, that perfect relationship, so you create it in your mind, "out of nothing at all" as the song goes. Your tears and your excessive needs that you believe you are not capable of filling while alone cause you to create illusions where unfortunately they can never be met because of a lack in each of you.

I have seen repeatedly that when this is the case, regardless of what is provided you haven't yet learned how to receive, on all levels, to a point of being filled. That is a skill that for many has never been developed. No matter how much is given it is never enough, or, they don't believe they are worthy so they don't allow themselves to feel full or seen. The vacuum they are experiencing inside remains regardless of their circumstances.

When you know that self-love and self-respect are required before you can get someone else to love and respect you fully, and that you must know how to fill your own needs, you may realize that there is a lot of work for you to do on you before you can enter a healthy relationship. No relationship can fill you. No relationship can replace self-love. No relationship can give you yourself and no one person can give you everything we need, no matter who he or she is. When you are grounded in that realization, there is no blame and no judgment about what your partner's skill sets are.

When you do enter another relationship you need to recognize all the needs that are not being met in your relationship, and create friendships that fill those needs. This is your responsibility. Perhaps one friend is the one that can help you explore your creative side in taking art classes or dance classes together etc.

Another friend could be the one you get to be glamorous with if that is not your partner's taste as the two of you spend a night once or twice a year in New York City for a play and a glamorous dinner out. All your needs can be met, even if not by your partner, but with a variety of friends you trust and enjoy. I say variety because truly, no one friend can fill all your needs either, no matter who he or she is.

It is such an important point to accept that friends are needed throughout your life for a variety of reasons. You may have one friend you can call on when you need an evening of pure laughter and silliness. This friend may have little or no desire for a deep thought in his or her life but have a great heart and a love of life that is contagious.

Another friend may be a joy and someone to share an afternoon of culture and shopping with along with intimate conversation. Another friend may always have a hug to give, an understanding, non-judgmental heart to share. With each one you will have a different kind of relationship, a different type of friendship but each can also be life-giving for the both of you.

When those friendships are in place and you know how to get your needs met in a healthy way, a lover, a friend, or a life-partner is a wonderful addition to your life. He or she brings you someone to love in a very different way. They bring you someone who will get to know you in a way no one else does. They will, hopefully, enter the inner sanctum of your heart and your soul. They will walk the path with you, beside you, and love you even when they don't like you at the moment. That is the relationship of a healthy dreamer.

The partner who will carry you, who will think you are perfect, who never ask anything of you, who only wants to give, is not a partner who will call you to grow, who will force you to learn to love, more and more, continuously, both of yourself and of him or her. That partner is an illusion. You deserve reality. You deserve true love. When you settle for the illusions, you never get to have your dreams.

- In what ways have you brought illusion into your relationships?
- In what ways have you refused to see your partners for who they were?
- In what ways have you pretended to be what you're not?
- Have you denied your needs or wants as if they didn't count so you could continue the illusion? Why? Did it work?

_____

_____

_____

_____

_____

_____

_____

_____

_____

_____

_____

_____

_____

In what ways have you refused to take responsibility for getting your needs met?

- In what way have you not shared a need and then blamed your partner for not filling it, believing that if he or she loved you enough s/he would know your needs and you would never need to express them?

_____

_____

_____

_____

_____

_____

_____

_____

_____

_____

_____

_____

_____

_____

_____

_____

_____

_____

_____

_____

_____

_____

_____

_____

_____

_____

- In what way do you set your partner up to fail by not sharing your dreams your visions and then feel that you are not supported in moving forward, in following those dreams?

_____

_____

_____

_____

_____

_____

_____

_____

_____

_____

_____

_____

_____

_____

_____

_____

_____

_____

_____

_____

_____

_____

_____

_____

_____
_____
_____
_____
_____
_____
_____
_____
_____
_____
_____
_____
_____
_____
_____
_____
_____
_____
_____
_____
_____
_____
_____
_____
_____
_____
_____
_____

- In what way do you play victim or powerless in relationship?
- In what ways do you refuse to participate fully?

_____

_____

_____

_____

_____

_____

_____

_____

_____

_____

_____

_____

_____

_____

_____

_____

_____

_____

_____

_____

_____

_____

_____

_____

_____

_____

_____

_____

_____

_____

Without you fully participating, the dream of a healthy relationship can never exist. You can never truly have a partnership of this type if both of you are not fully invested.

- In what way do you passively wait for your partner to take control of a situation, an aspect of your lives together, or even of your social life and then blame him or her for always wanting things their way?

_____
_____
_____
_____
_____
_____
_____
_____
_____
_____
_____
_____
_____
_____
_____
_____
_____
_____
_____
_____

- If you were to sit back and take an objective look at your relationship, what would you change?
- Add?
- Subtract?
- What are you willing to do to create that?

_____
_____
_____
_____
_____
_____
_____
_____
_____
_____
_____
_____
_____
_____
_____
_____
_____
_____
_____
_____
_____
_____
_____
_____

For those of you who have chosen not to be in a relationship at the moment, why did you make that choice? The truth is important to confront without justification. Simply understand the reality of your choice not the message you want to convey to others.

It could be for a very healthy reason. Perhaps you have recently left a relationship and you need to take time so assess what happened, how you may have contributed to its not working or its ending.

If you are recently widowed you will need time to grieve and to reassess what you want in a partner and in a relationship at this point in your life. You will need to look closely at who you have become through this marriage and through the death process.

It is important when a relationship ends, for whatever reason, that you take the time to rediscover you, to assess where you want to go in your life, and to become comfortable in your own skin as a separate, single entity. Until you have done that you are not capable of bringing in a healthy relationship, instead it would be one based on need or fear. Neither you nor your partner deserves that.

You may also be in the midst of a major life change in terms of location, job, children coming home or leaving, or a major new project at work that requires all your attention as you implement the necessary logistics. Any of these and other reasons are important to honor. It is important however to acknowledge when these reasons later become excuses because of fear, anger, depression, or a lack of self-worth.

If the latter is the case:

- What unresolved issues exist from your previous relationship?
- What is your image of the opposite sex (or same sex partners if that is your preference.)?
- Do you doubt your ability to choose a healthy partner based on past patterns?
- What are your past patterns? If you notice you keep dating the same type and the relationships never work, what are you not seeing about your choices? Your expectations?

_____

_____

_____

_____

_____

_____

_____

_____

_____

_____

_____

_____

_____

_____

_____

_____

_____

_____

_____

_____

_____

- Who in your past do these partners remind you of?
- Can you become a partner in your relationship rather than a parent or a child?
- A participant rather than a victim?

_____
_____
_____
_____
_____
_____
_____
_____
_____
_____
_____
_____
_____
_____
_____
_____
_____
_____
_____
_____
_____
_____
_____
_____
_____
_____

Fear, anger and blame are not uncommon when past relationships have failed or not lived up to our expectations. It can be disappointing even heart-breaking for a while, but when we refuse to learn from it, to see our role in it, in choosing the partner we did we lose the opportunity for growth provided. We then don't learn what we need to know about ourselves in order to make a healthier choice next time.

You may feel you pick a wide variety of partners but if the same issues exist in each relationship, the problems are not with your partners but with the criteria you use in choosing them. After assessing your patterns, become the woman or man you want to be to have the kind of relationship you want to have. Healthy people choose healthy partners. Look at what is missing in your expectations and increase them to find a partner who is at your level or slightly above. Then you will need to open yourself for more learning but in a more loving and more embracing environment.

All dreams are meant to be lived, including our dream relationship. But relationships are not illusions, they are not one-sided, and they require us to be fully invested, fully present in creating them and in maintaining them. We cannot put our dreams on another and passively wait, expecting them to come true.

Only through your guidance, in openly sharing your hopes, wants and needs can another address them, talk about them and try to work with you to make them happen. Ultimately, however, it is your responsibility. You have entered a relationship with another human, another fallible human being at that. The best you can ask is that they try, that they honestly try. You deserve that. They also deserve the right to be human, never cruel or abusive, but always human.

In this mix of two sets of dreams and expectations there are times when something falls by the wayside. What you do with that defines your ability and your willingness to be in relationship. This isn't about blame or the good guys or the bad guys. It is about two human beings trying to be there for each other while remaining true to themselves.

At times, what falls by the wayside can be picked up and taken to a friend to be filled, or to be shared. At times, what gets lost is the basis of the relationship. You need to know the difference. When you choose a partner to walk through life with, no matter who they are, they will not grow in the same way or at the same time as you. To expect that is unfair. There are two separate journeys here. There are two separate people, each living their own life, choosing to share it with the other. It takes work; it takes commitment and it takes focus, just like any other dream.

A basic expectation must be that the relationship will change and it will change many times. As you change, you change what you bring to the relationship. You change what you expect of the relationship. As a result, you need to keep the changes open and present to your partner. How else can they adapt and change with you? If you don't stay present, how can you blame them for not following? If you don't share the changes within you, how can you expect them to understand?

For some, there is a time when one partner chooses not to grow any more. They may choose not to accept certain growths in their partner. They may choose not to be present any longer. There can be any number of reasons for that choice. Regardless of the reason, when one or both partners permanently choose not to be present any longer, the relationship ceases to exist.

If you are to live in your truth, you must continue to grow. Fear of leaving a dead relationship comes when you believe you are incapable of making it on your own. It comes when you believe you can never be loved again. It comes when you believe this relationship, not you, was the reason for your living.

None of these beliefs are real. They are simply fear and the excuses you hold onto to stay safe, to stay in the known. Choosing safety is choosing death. Safety creates stagnation. Stagnation causes infestation and death. It is an absolute form of self-betrayal.

You are never alone. You may have simply not chosen to see all the support that has brought into your life when you needed it most. Notice that when you accept that it is time to leave all kinds of new friends and support show up in your life. I hear it constantly from patients. It is not coincidental. Others have been waiting. Once you choose to take that risk, they come to prepare the path, as always.

You must continue to follow your dreams. They are the reason you are here. They are the reconnection to your heart and soul. However you do it, wherever you do it, you deserve to be loved, supported, and nurtured. In or out of a special relationship you need to bring these elements into your life. Friends can do that. Family can do that and you can do that. You need to believe you deserve it before you reach out for it however. Believe me you deserve all this and so much more...

Chapter Seven

The Rest of Our Lives

Throughout our lives we will continue to create dreams, the dream vacation, the dream home, the dream career, and again, the dream relationship, if we allow ourselves. We deserve all of them. We need all of them if we are to become all that we are meant to be. As always the question is "Are you willing to pay the price?" You alone can make that decision.

It is important to realize that for the rest of your life you will be in transition. For the rest of your life you will be changing, growing, and needing to adapt to all of it. Many transitions we are spearheading, we are designing, consciously or unconsciously. Why not do so consciously? Other transitions are thrust upon us, such as those resulting from world events, or from the impact of another's dream. Regardless of the cause, transition is a way of life as we grow and change whether in response to or in reaction to events within or around us.

In each new situation you need to begin again. You need to reevaluate where you are, where you want to go, and who you want to become. You need to take the time for prayer, meditation, and reflection so that you are listening to what your heart and soul is telling you. You need to be conscious of what you are called to next. It may be something you never would have considered under different circumstances. Yet, now, here you are being called yet again to call up more of you, becoming even more than you realized was possible

I have seen widows and widowers and those divorced after 40 years of marriage literally sway in shock when their new reality first hit. I have seen them later, when they have started to come out of the shock, be saddened by what has happened yet realize they now have experiences they never could have imagined if they were still married. Honoring their need to adjust over time, in waves perhaps, they came to discover dreams they thought were long forgotten. They took up kayaking, travel, a cruise, a move to a smaller and more enjoyable house.

They accepted their new reality and allowed themselves to dream again finding a self they never knew existed. They discovered independence, a sense of adventure and a self they never took the time to know.

I have seen the same with many who have retired. They had created a dream of what this time of life would look like yet it didn't feel at all like they imagined. When they adjusted to this shock, in bewilderment, and with support, they allowed themselves to find another dream, another sense of who they were and what they wanted from life. With that came another dream, one they never thought they would want or need and yet one their whole life had been preparing them for.

Where ever you are in your life, whatever stage you are at, remember that your dreams are not a luxury; they are an absolute necessity. They are your present and your future. If you permit yourself to stay stuck you are betraying all that you are called to be.

Living in the Caribbean and walking the beach on a regular basis, I often saw a lot of tourists who were surprised that I lived there. They wanted to know how I got to be so "lucky." They would tell me that it was their dream to live in the Caribbean. They would tell me that they envied me and my life. When I would tell them if they wanted to live there they simply needed to move down. They would tell me they couldn't since they had a family. I would say calmly "So do I." "I have children." "So do I." "I own a house." "So did I." They could go on and on with all of the excuses as to why their dream could never come true. In reality, if they really wanted that dream, and were willing to pay the price, it would be theirs.

Unfortunately, so many people live with a belief that they cannot have their dreams or that dreams are irresponsible. They believe that dreams can only be justified after they have filled all forms of never-ending responsibilities and demands. As a result, they may live their life with "If only..." as their refrain. How sad.

Every dream cost something. It all depends upon whether or not it is worth the cost to you. If it isn't that is OK but accept that reality. If you find someone else has a really nice dream and has made it, be happy for them and tell them. If it isn't your dream, that is OK. There is no one "right" dream. We are all called to walk different journeys, enjoy yours. The search can give you something to look forward to, something to prepare for, to grow into. It will keep your passion and your vibrancy alive and that is what keeps you healthy and your body alive as well.

On the other hand, to walk through life saying "If only..." leaves you in a negative energy pattern of powerlessness and of playing the victim. "Poor me" is a very sad way of living your journey. It is important to realize as well that the cost of that mentality could be your health, on all levels including emotionally, spiritually, and physically.

- How often do you say or feel "If only..." or "poor me..." or "I wish..."?
- Why do you limit yourself?

_____

_____

_____

_____

_____

_____

_____

_____

_____

_____

_____

_____

_____

_____

_____

_____

_____

_____

- What belief are you building that on?
- Where did it come from?

_____
_____
_____
_____
_____
_____
_____
_____
_____
_____
_____
_____
_____
_____
_____
_____
_____
_____
_____
_____
_____
_____
_____
_____
_____
_____
_____
_____
_____

- Do you have a dream at this moment?
- If so, what is it?
- If not, what would it be if you had one?

_____

_____

_____

_____

_____

_____

_____

_____

_____

_____

_____

_____

_____

_____

_____

_____

_____

_____

_____

_____

_____

_____

_____

_____

_____

_____

We don't have all the answers available to us. We don't even have all the questions, not yet. They will come when we are ready. In the meantime we are called to live in our truth, in our integrity, and to follow our dreams as they appear. It means taking the time to listen as I have said often throughout this workbook, listening in the silence to your heart and your soul calling you forward.

If you don't know what your dreams are, consider these questions - one at a time.

- What is it that fills your heart to pounding?
- What is it that makes you want to get up in the morning?
- What is it that makes you want to dance around the room?
- Most importantly, what is it that makes you feel most like you, more alive and more grateful to be here than you have ever been?

_____
_____
_____
_____
_____
_____
_____
_____
_____
_____
_____
_____
_____

If you don't know, learn to go within. Learn to listen to your soul. It has all the answers AND all the questions, all you need to do is learn to hear them. Anything is possible, just try, and then reach for the stars while you are doing it. You don't deserve any less.

God bless and may all your dreams come true!

Dr. Dorothy A. Martin-Neville can be reached at:
Email: dorothy@drdorothyct.com
Website: www.drdorothyct.com
Phone: 860-461-7569